HAUNTED PLACES

HAUNTED HOTELS

KENNY ABDO

Fly!
An Imprint of Abdo Zoom
abdobooks.com

abdobooks.com

Published by Abdo Zoom, a division of ABDO, P.O. Box 398166, Minneapolis, Minnesota 55439. Copyright © 2021 by Abdo Consulting Group, Inc. International copyrights reserved in all countries. No part of this book may be reproduced in any form without written permission from the publisher. Fly!™ is a trademark and logo of Abdo Zoom.

Printed in the United States of America, North Mankato, Minnesota.
052020
092020

Photo Credits: Alamy, AP Images, Flickr, iStock, Newscom, North Wind Picture Archives, Shutterstock, ©City of Boston Archives p11 / CC BY 2.0, ©Victorgrigas p14 / CC BY-SA 3.0, ©Richard Martin p16 / CC BY 2.0
Production Contributors: Kenny Abdo, Jennie Forsberg, Grace Hansen
Design Contributors: Dorothy Toth, Neil Klinepier

Library of Congress Control Number: 2019956196

Publisher's Cataloging-in-Publication Data

Names: Abdo, Kenny, author.
Title: Haunted hotels / by Kenny Abdo
Description: Minneapolis, Minnesota : Abdo Zoom, 2021 | Series: Haunted places | Includes online resources and index.
Identifiers: ISBN 9781098221317 (lib. bdg.) | ISBN 9781644944127 (pbk.) | ISBN 9781098222291 (ebook) | ISBN 9781098222789 (Read-to-Me ebook)
Subjects: LCSH: Haunted places--Juvenile literature. | Haunted hotels--Juvenile literature. | Ghosts--Juvenile literature. | Haunted houses--Juvenile literature.
Classification: DDC 133.122--dc23

TABLE OF CONTENTS

Hotels. 4

The History 8

The Haunted 12

The Media 20

Glossary 22

Online Resources 23

Index 24

HOTELS

Hotels, as we know them, have been around since the 1700s. In that time, an unlucky few have never checked out.

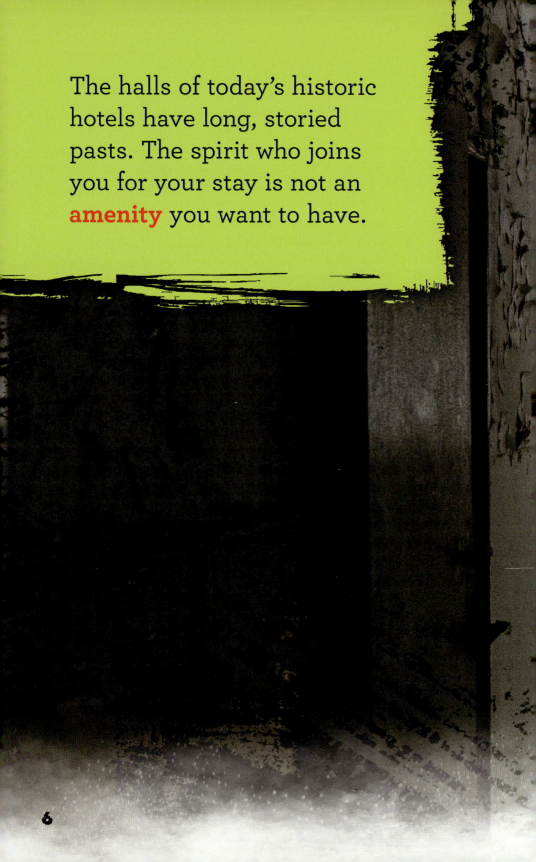

The halls of today's historic hotels have long, storied pasts. The spirit who joins you for your stay is not an **amenity** you want to have.

THE HISTORY

Hotels have been around since the early years of **civilization**. During the Greek and Roman **eras**, **lodging** would be set up for travelers passing through.

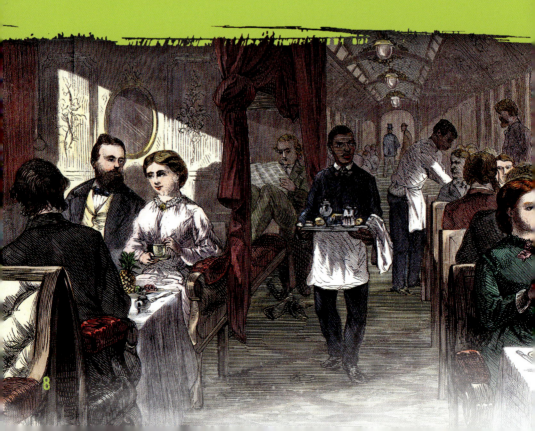

Throughout the centuries, **lodgings** began to spring up around the world. By the 17th century, coaching inns became popular.

The Tremont House opened in Boston in 1829. It was the first modern hotel in the United States. Today, the hotel industry is strong. Some places even offer their guests evening frights and sleepless nights.

THE HAUNTED

Dragsholm Slot was a beautiful castle built in Denmark in the 12th century. Over time, it turned into a hotel of nightmares. It is said to be haunted by two women and the **Earl of Bothwell**. He was imprisoned in the cellars during the late 1500s.

In 1716, Concord's Colonial Inn opened in Massachusetts. During the **Revolutionary War**, it was used as a hospital. Room 424 was once an operating room. Many guests have reported hauntings in that room.

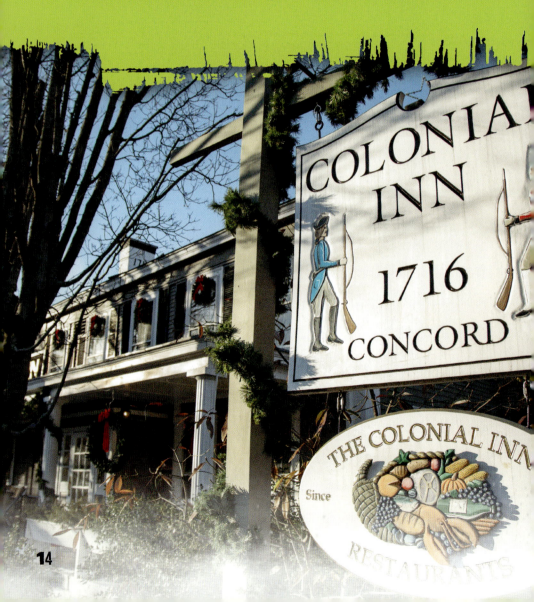

The Karosta Hostel was first a **Nazi** prison. Thousands of prisoners died there. Modern guests say they have seen doors open by themselves. They've also seen the ghost of a woman wandering its corridors.

The Bourbon Orleans Hotel was originally an orphanage. After the **yellow fever** wiped out most of the children, it was shut down. Today, guests have seen the ghosts of nuns chasing children throughout the hotel.

Built in 1909, the Stanley Hotel is the most famous haunted hotel in America. Guests have heard suspicious piano music and voices during their stay.

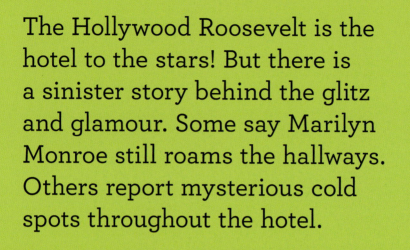

The Hollywood Roosevelt is the hotel to the stars! But there is a sinister story behind the glitz and glamour. Some say Marilyn Monroe still roams the hallways. Others report mysterious cold spots throughout the hotel.

THE MEDIA

Author Stephen King was so spooked during his stay at the Stanley Hotel, he wrote *The Shining*. The film, based on King's novel, was released in 1980.

Book a room at one of these hotels if you dare. There are many to choose from for a good scare.

GLOSSARY

amenity – a feature that brings comfort, convenience, or enjoyment.

American Revolution – (1775 to 1783) A war for independence between Great Britain and its North American colonies. The colonists won and created the United States of America.

civilization – a well-organized and advanced society.

earl – a British nobleman.

era – a period of time or history.

lodging – a room rented out where someone lives or stays briefly.

Nazi – a member of the political party that controlled Germany under Adolf Hitler from 1933 to 1945.

yellow fever – a virus transmitted by mosquitoes in warm climates. It is marked by chills, fever, headache, and yellow-colored skin.

ONLINE RESOURCES

To learn more about haunted hotels, please visit **abdobooklinks.com** or scan this QR code. These links are routinely monitored and updated to provide the most current information available.

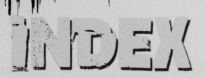
INDEX

Bourbon Orleans Hotel 16

coaching inns 10

Concord's Colonial Inn 14

Denmark 13

Dragsholm Slot 13

Hollywood Roosevelt Hotel 18

Karsota Hostel 15

King, Stephen 20

Massachusetts 11, 14

Monroe, Marilyn 18

Revolutionary War 14

Shining, The 20

Stanley Hotel 17, 20

Tremont House, The 11